ROSSY ZAPATA

THE BOOK OF 100 DRAGONS

A FANTASY-THEMED COLORING BOOK

For information and new releases, please visit www.rossyzapata.com

THIS BOOK BELONGS TO:

HORIZONTAL FORMAT

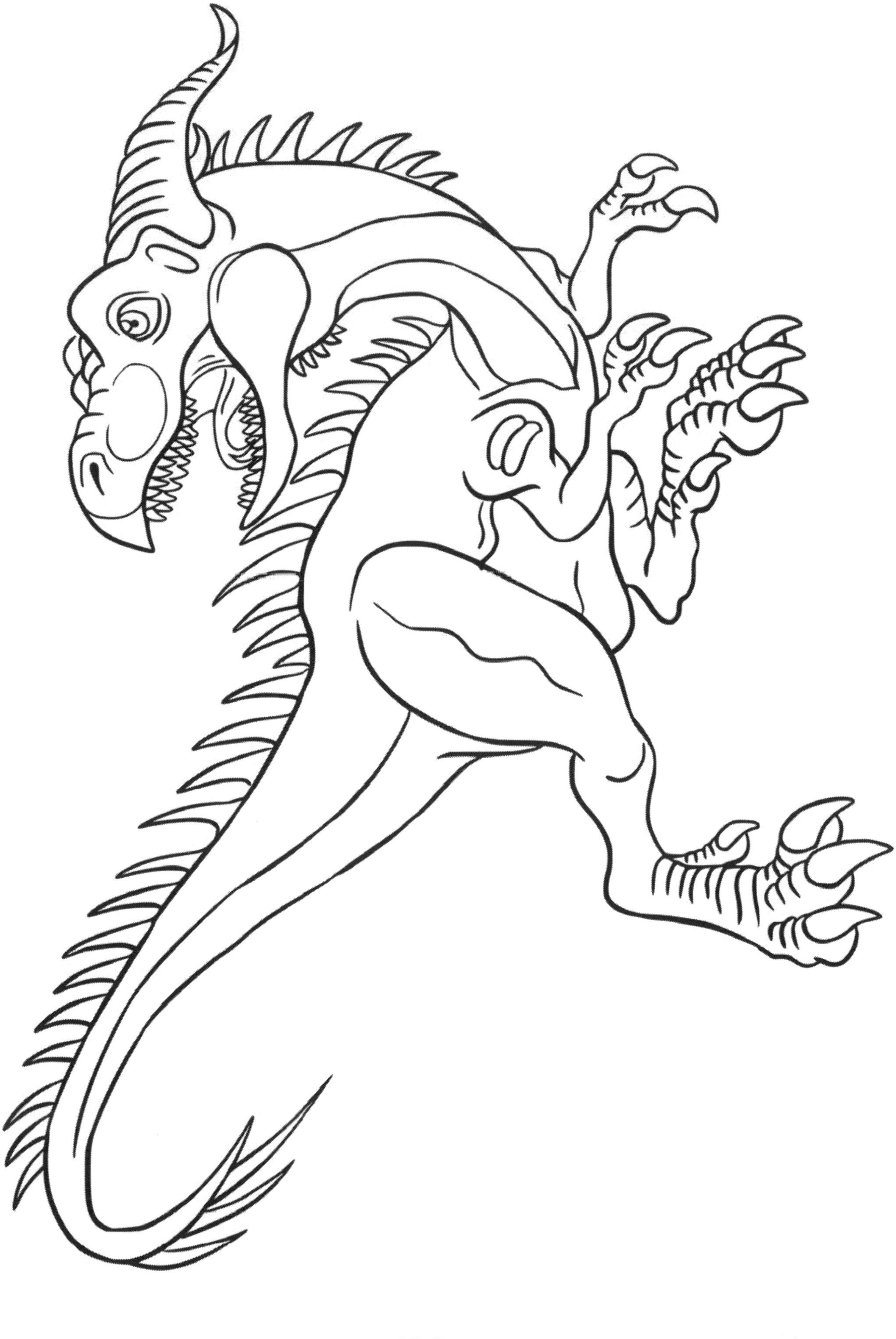

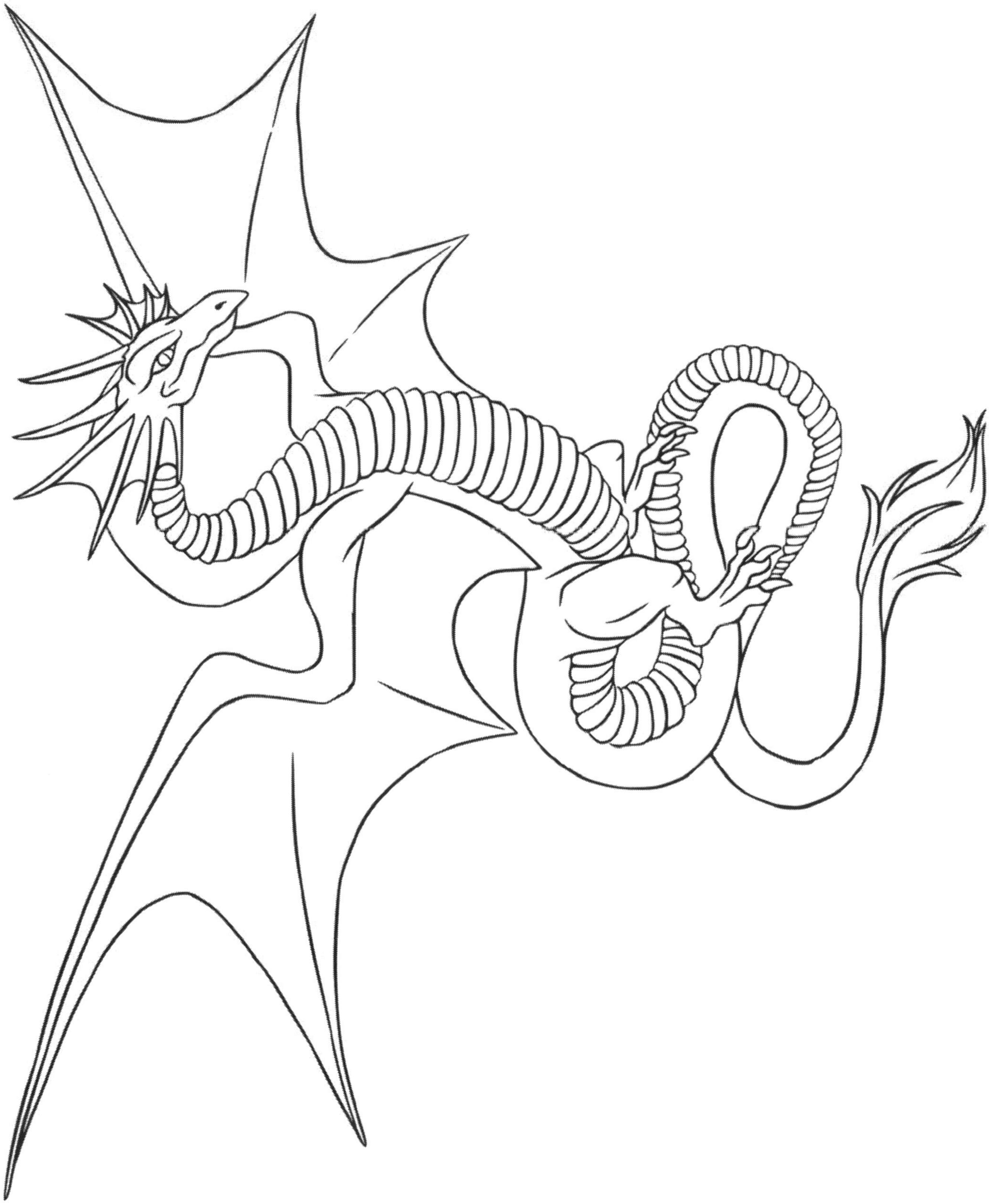

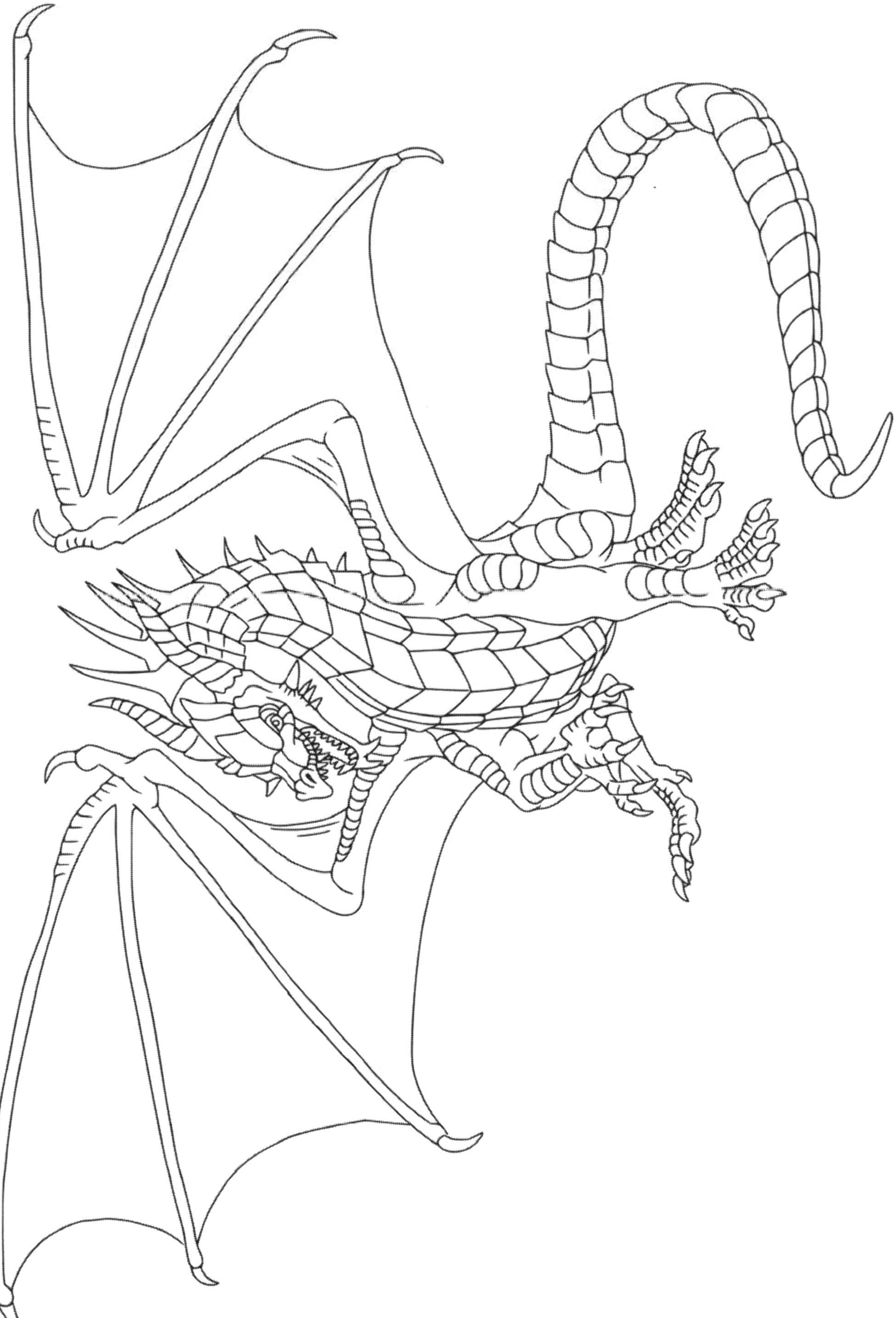

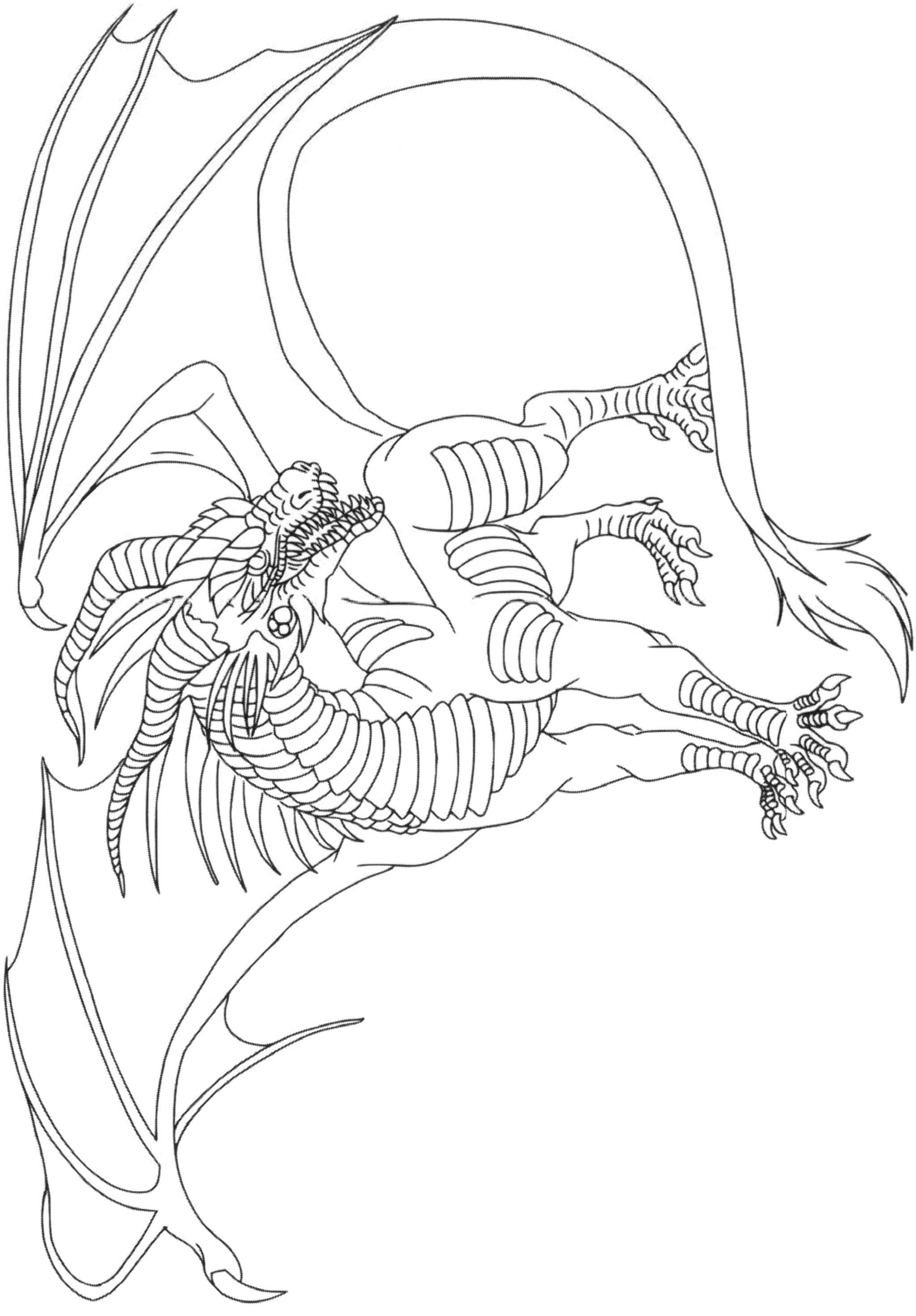

34702253R00126

Made in the USA
Columbia, SC
17 November 2018